Dancing

Donna Bailey

STECK-VAUGHN
L I B R A R Y
A Division of Steck-Vaughn Company

I am learning to dance.
First our class does an exercise
to make our feet and ankles stronger.
We sit on the floor and point our toes
up and down in time to the music.

2

Now, we lie on our backs and lift up
each leg in time to the music.
This will help us lift our legs higher
when we learn to do kicks.

When we sit up, we do an exercise
to make our tummies stronger.
We hold our arms out in front of
us and sit up slowly.

We listen hard to the
rhythm of the music.
We clap our hands to mark the rhythm.

Then we march in time to the music.
We swing our arms and pretend
we are marching in a parade.

6

Now the music has changed.
It has a bouncy rhythm.
We jump up and down to the music
and pretend to be bouncing balls.

We learn lots of dance steps.
Here we are doing spring kicks
to the music.
We lift our legs as high as we can.

Our teacher shows me how to
hold out my arms.
Now, I can balance better.

We learn an important dance step
called step-ball-change.
We also learn to do step-dips.

10

Our teacher says we must
feel what the music tells us.
We express what the music
is saying to each of us.

One of my friends pretends to be dead.
We show our teacher how sad we feel.

Now our teacher plays a happy tune.
We try to look as funny as possible.

Then the older girls begin warming up.
They are doing an exercise to make
their body and legs more limber.
This exercise helps them do the splits.

Our teacher shows them
how to stand.
The girls work on a special pose.

Exercises and practice have
made the girls limber.
Their pose shows how they
have learned to work together.

Dancers listen to
the rhythms of the music.
They try to tell the story of
the music through movements.

Dancers often copy the movements
of animals and birds.
These dancers are pretending
to be chickens.

18

Many movies, musical plays,
and revues have dancers.
These dancers are in the musical play
"Starlight Express."

The scenery, make-up, and costumes
all help tell the story of the dance.
Do you know which story this dance tells?

20

Many of the steps that
dancers use are linked to
folk and ethnic dance.
These African dancers use the rhythm
of the drums to guide their steps.

Flamenco dancers in Spain play
castanets as they dance.
They move their feet to the rhythm
of the castanets.

This Indian dancer has bells around
her ankles.
She makes the bells ring as
she dances.

Indian dancers use their body, their legs,
and their hands to tell a story.
This dancer's pose tells us
she is playing a flute.

Some Indian dancers train for many years.
They spend their lives singing and
dancing in the temples.

The long fingernails of this Thai dancer
tell us that she is a princess.
Thai dancers use their hands, feet, and
arms to give messages.

26

Japanese dancers use their fans
to tell stories.
An open fan may show that the dancer
is telling about the sun or the moon.

Noh dancers of Japan wear wooden masks
and fancy costumes.
Each small movement in their dance
means something special.

Folk dances usually have special meanings.
These dragon dancers hope to
bring good luck at Chinese New Year.

These dancers in Bali are doing
a barong dance to keep
their village safe.

These Native Americans are dancing
to celebrate the coming of spring.

During harvest festival in Poland,
dancers show thanks for the harvest.
Music and dancing are important
all around the world.

Index

African dancers, 21
arms 4, 6, 9, 26
balance 9, 16
Bali 30
barong dance 30
bells 23
castanets 22
dragon dancers 29
drums 21
ethnic dance 21
exercises 2, 4, 14
fans 27
feelings 12, 13
feet 2, 26
fingernails 26
Flamenco dancers 22
folk dances 21, 29

hands 5, 24, 26
harvest dance 32
Indian dancers 23, 24, 25
Japanese dancers 27, 28
legs 3, 8, 14, 24
marching 6
masks 28
movements 17, 18
music 2, 3, 5, 6, 7, 8, 11, 17
musicals 19
Native Americans 31
Noh dancers 28
poses 15, 16, 24
rhythm 5, 7, 17, 21, 22
steps 8, 10
Thai dancers 26

Editorial Consultant: Donna Bailey
Executive Editor: Elizabeth Strauss
Project Editor: Becky Ward

Picture research by Jennifer Garratt
Designed by Richard Garratt Design

Photographs
All photographs by Peter Greenland except:
Dance Library: 17, 18, 19, 20, 28 (Darryl Williams); 24 (Nick Sidle); 30 (Derek Richards); 31
Hutchison Library: 21; 25, 26 (Michael Macintyre); 29 (Trevor Page)
Robert Harding: 22, 23 (Chananda J. Highet); 27 (Carol Jopp); 32 (Chris Niendenthal)

Library of Congress Cataloging-in-Publication Data: Bailey, Donna.
Dancing / Donna Bailey. p. cm.—(Sports world) Includes index. Summary: Looks at the different kinds of
dance steps, rhythms, and exercises for dancers, and the ethnic origins of dancing.   ISBN 0-8114-2902-4
1. Dance—Juvenile literature. 2. Dancing—Juvenile literature. [1. Dance. 2. Dancing.] I. Title. II. Series:
Bailey, Donna. Sports World. GV1783.B35 1991 792.8—dc 20 90-23057 CIP AC